Creepy Creatures

Centipedes

Nancy Dickmann

Raintree

Chicago, Illinois

Printed and bound by South China Printing Company.
10 09 08 07 06
10 9 8 7 6 5 4 3 2 1

Library of Congress Cataloging-in-Publication Data:
Dickmann, Nancy.
  Centipedes / Nancy Dickmann.
    p. cm. -- (Creepy creatures)
  Includes index.
  ISBN 1-4109-1768-1 (library binding - hardcover) -- ISBN 1-4109-1773-8 (pbk.)
  1. Centipedes--Juvenile literature. I. Title. II. Series.

QL449.5.D53 2006
595.6'2--dc22
                                                         2005012451

Acknowledgments
The publishers would like to thank the following for permission to reproduce photographs: Corbis p. **20**
(Gary W Carter); FLPA pp. **8–9** (D Jones), **12** (Tom Vezo); Getty Images pp. **10–11** (National Geographic);
Natural Visions pp. **21** (Franceso Tomasinelli), **22** (Heather Angel); Nature Picture Library p. **23**; Oxford
Scientific Films pp. **4** (Animals Animals/Daybreak Imagery), **5** (Animals Animals/Daybreak Imagery), **6, 7, 13,**
14–15 (Satoshi Kuribayashi), **16** (Satoshi Kuribayashi), **17** (Zig Leszczynski), **18** (Satoshi Kuribayashi), **23**;
Science Photo Library **18**.

Cover picture of a centipede reproduced with permission of Oxford Scientific Films/Animals Animals.

Every effort has been made to contact copyright holders of any material reproduced in this book.
Any omissions will be rectified in subsequent printings if notice is given to the publishers.

Some words are shown in bold, **like this**. You can find out what they mean by looking in the glossary on page 24.

Contents

Centipedes

Centipedes are **long** and thin.

They have
lots and lots
of legs.

Looking for Centipedes

You might find a centipede on an old piece of wood.

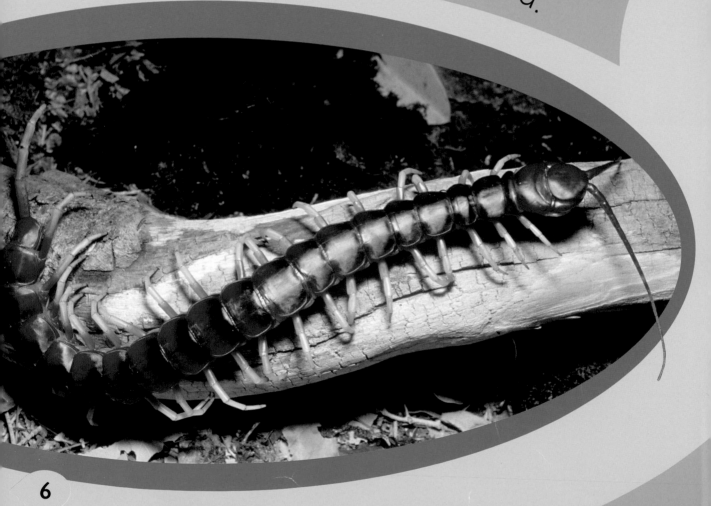

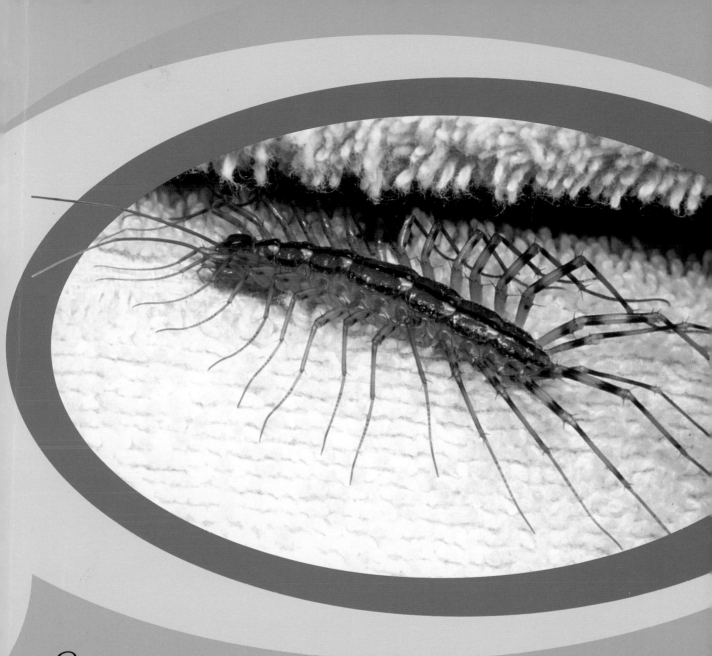

Sometimes they hide in our homes.

A Centipede's Body

A centipede's body has many **segments**.

Each segment has two legs.

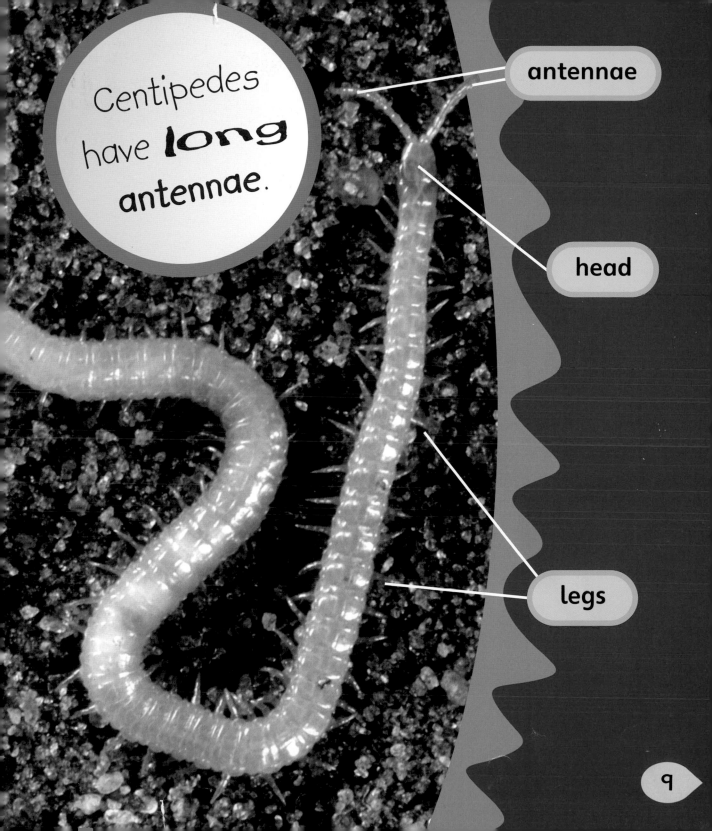

Centipedes have **long** antennae.

antennae

head

legs

A Centipede's Legs

Some centipedes have 30 legs.

Some have more than 300!

If a centipede loses a leg, it can regrow it.

Centipedes on the Move

Centipedes are *fast*.

Some can run backward!

They use their **antennae**
to feel their way.

Centipede Eggs

A female centipede lays her eggs.

She hides them in the soil.

Young Centipedes

Baby centipedes **hatch**
from the eggs.

As they get bigger, they get *longer.*

They grow more legs.

Food for Centipedes

Centipedes
hunt at night.

They catch spiders and small insects to eat.

Yum!

Centipedes in Danger

Birds and toads like to eat centipedes.

Some centipedes cannot run fast enough to get away.

21

Types of Centipedes

There are thousands of different kinds of centipedes.

Glossary

antenna (More than one are antennae.) *feeler on an insect's head that helps it smell, see, or hear*

hatch *to come out of an egg*

segment *small sections that make up a centipede's body*

Index

Notes for Adults

This series supports the young child's exploration of their learning environment and their knowledge and understanding of their world. Using the books in the series together will enable comparison of similarities and differences to be made. (NB. Many of the photographs in **Creepy Creatures** show them much larger than life size. The first spread of each title shows the creature at approximately its real life size.)

This book introduces the reader to the life cycle and behavior of the centipede. It will also help children extend their vocabulary as they hear new words like *segment*, *antennae*, and *hatch*. You may like to introduce and explain other new words yourself, like *larva*, *habitat*, and *molt*.

Additional Information

Centipedes are arthropods, not insects. They have long, thin jointed bodies with a head and many segments, each with a pair of legs. "Centipede" means "100 legs" but they can have anywhere from 15 to 175 pairs. The first set of legs, below the mouth, are adapted into "poison jaws" for killing prey. Centipedes have poor eyesight and use their antennae and bristles on hind legs to find their way around. Centipedes have only 14 legs when they hatch. As they grow they molt repeatedly and grow new segments and legs. They chase down prey and paralyze it with venomous claws. There are about 2,800 species of centipedes, including soil-dwellers and rock-dwellers; they range in size from 5 mm to 30 cm.

Follow-up Activities

Can the children think of other animals or insects with many legs?

• Think about how an animal with so many legs moves around. Try to copy its movements.
• Draw, paint, or make models of centipedes.
• Read a fictional story such as *Centipede's One Hundred Shoes* by Tony Ross, and ask the children to relate the events to factual information in this book.

24